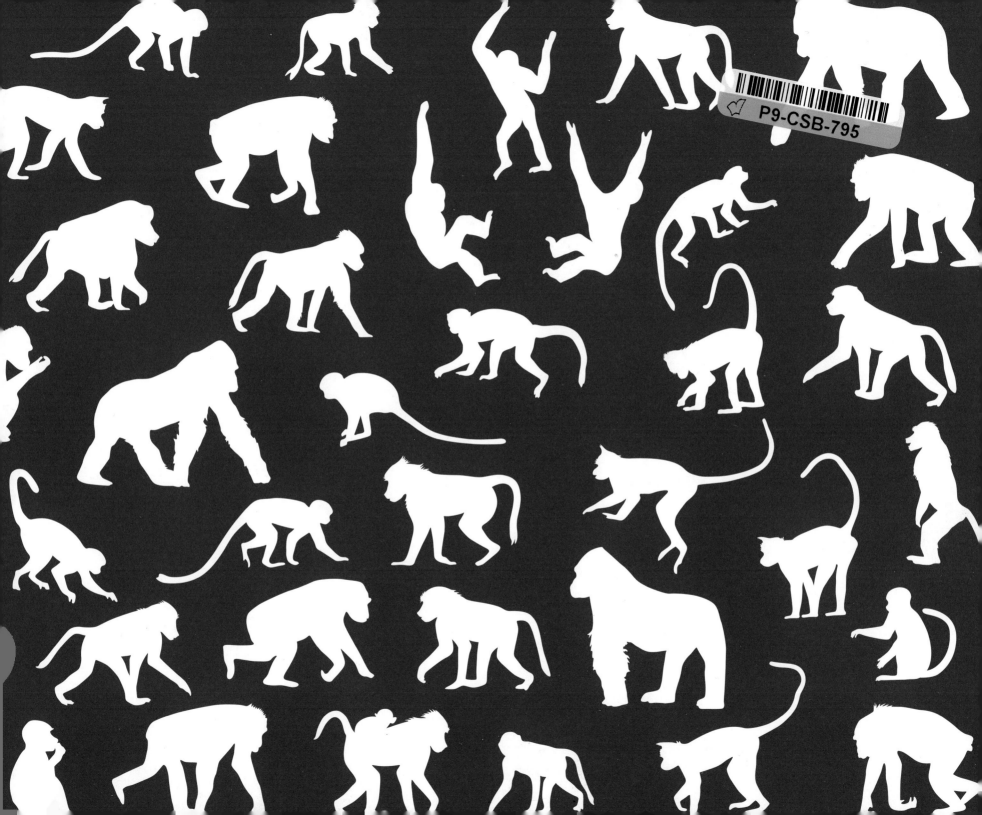

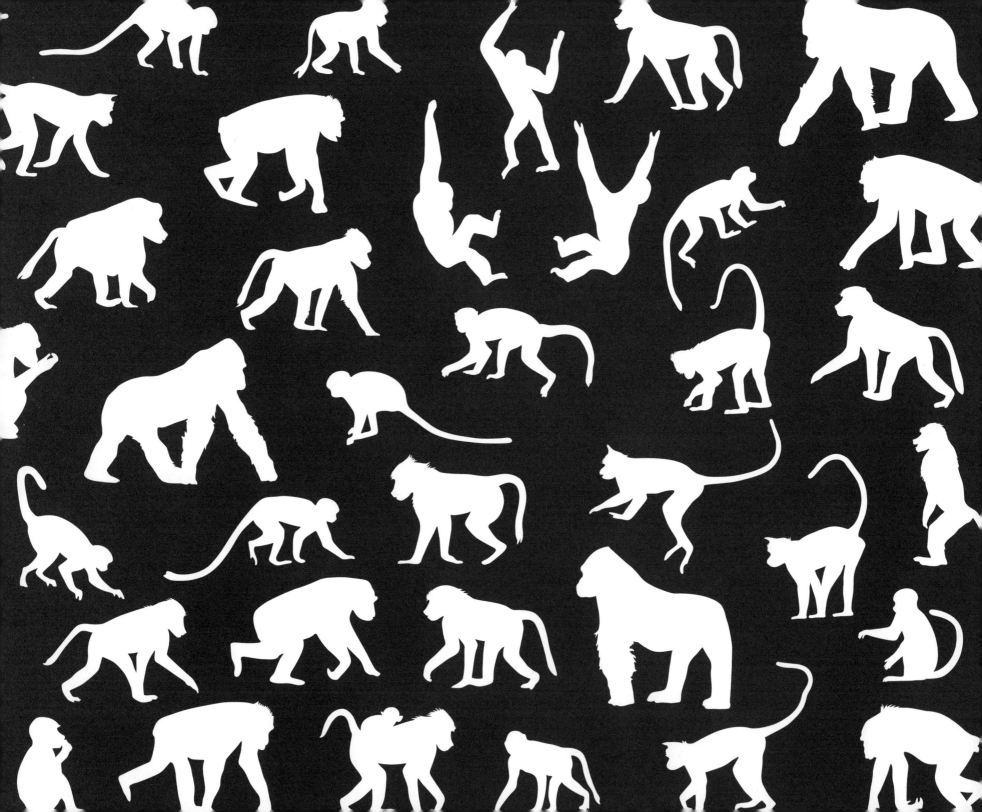

NATIONAL
GEOGRAPHIC
KiDS

You Can Be a
Primatologist!

Jill Pruetz, Ph.D.

NATIONAL GEOGRAPHIC
WASHINGTON, D.C.

What Is a Primatologist?

Hi! My name is Jill Pruetz, and I'm a primatologist.

A primatologist studies primates such as lemurs, monkeys, tarsiers, and apes.

I STUDY HOW CHIMPS BEHAVE. THEY USE STICKS LIKE THIS ONE AS TOOLS.

I study chimpanzees that live on the African savanna. Scientists know a lot about how chimps live in many other places. But I want to know how they live here.

I have been interested in animals my whole life. When I was growing up in Texas, U.S.A., my family always had pets. Now I have pet dogs. And I just added two cows to my family! But I didn't know much about primates until I learned about them in school. I was hooked.

Are you curious about animals? Do you want to learn about chimps and other primates?

Come along on my adventure!

I STUDY CHIMPS LIKE THIS ONE.

Do Primatologists Live Near the Animals They Study?

Most primates live in the tropics. These warm, wet areas often have jungles. Primates can also live in woodlands, swamps, or forests where it sometimes snows. Some primates, like the chimpanzees I study, live on savannas that include both grasslands and woodlands.

Primatologists who study these animals live in these places, too! We want to watch and learn about primates in their natural homes. Primatologists also work at zoos or animal sanctuaries. Some are professors at universities. They study primates and also teach classes. That way more people can learn about these amazing animals.

The chimpanzees I study live only in Africa. When my team and I are studying them in the field, we live in thatched huts in a small village called Fongoli in the country of Senegal. We don't have running water. But we do have solar power, which lets us charge a single lightbulb for each of the five huts that make up our camp inside the village. Fongoli is more than 5,000 miles (8,000 km) from my home in Texas!

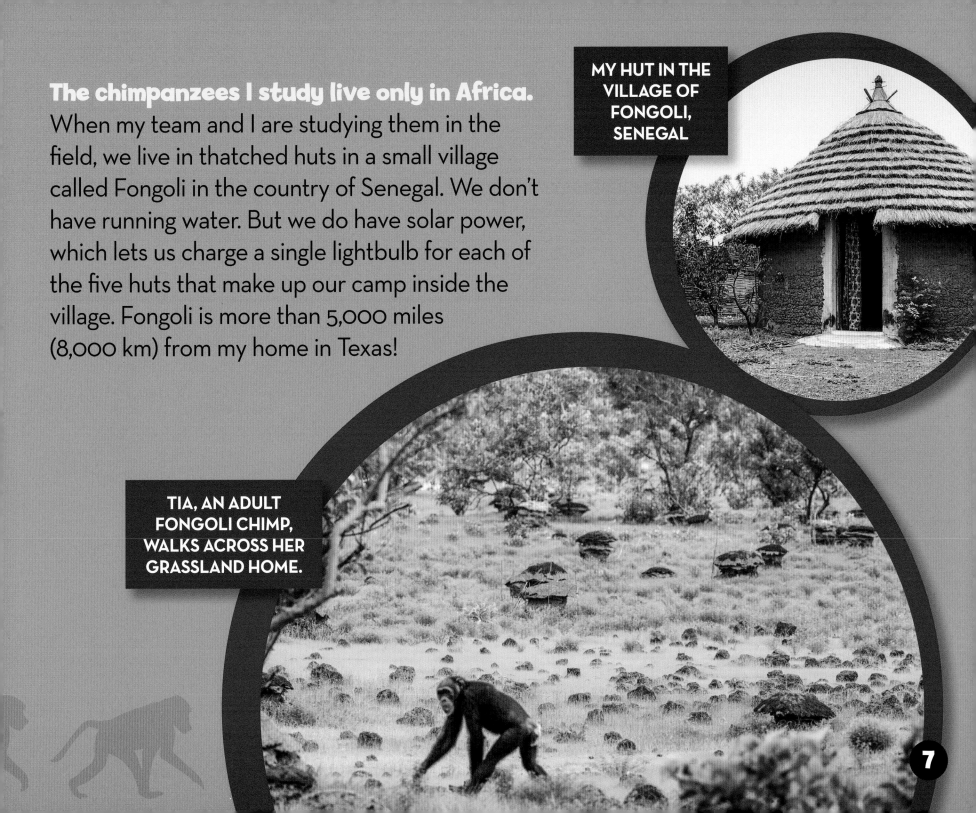

MY HUT IN THE VILLAGE OF FONGOLI, SENEGAL

TIA, AN ADULT FONGOLI CHIMP, WALKS ACROSS HER GRASSLAND HOME.

What Are Some Different Types of Primates?

mouse lemur

ring-tailed lemur

Primates are usually divided into groups: **lemurs** and their relatives, **tarsiers, monkeys,** and **apes.** Primates can be as small as a mouse lemur, which weighs no more than a slice of bread. Or they can be as big as an Eastern lowland gorilla. A male Eastern lowland gorilla can be about half the weight of a horse. The chimps I study at Fongoli are in between. They can weigh from 80 to 100 pounds (36 to 45 kg), and the alpha, or leader, comes up to my shoulder if he's standing on two legs.

How do you tell apes and monkeys apart? If it doesn't have a tail, it's an ape!

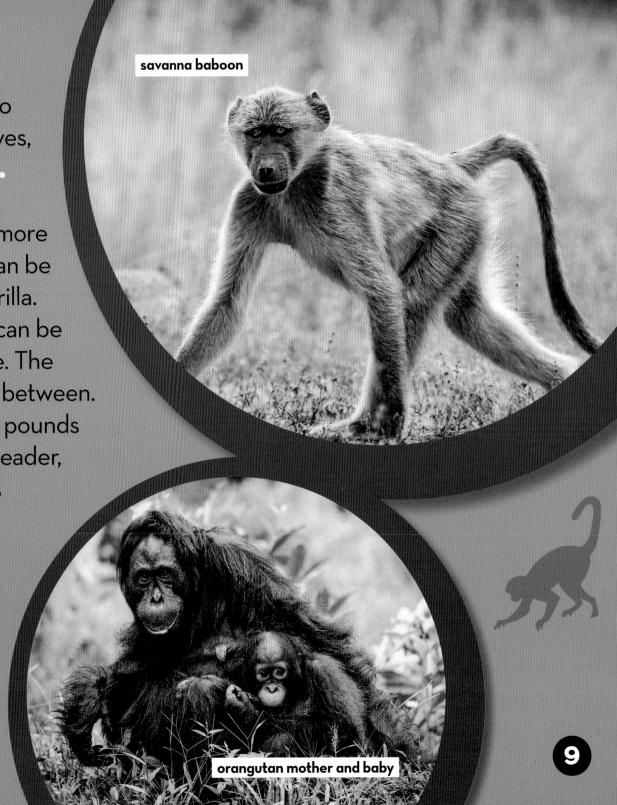

savanna baboon

orangutan mother and baby

9

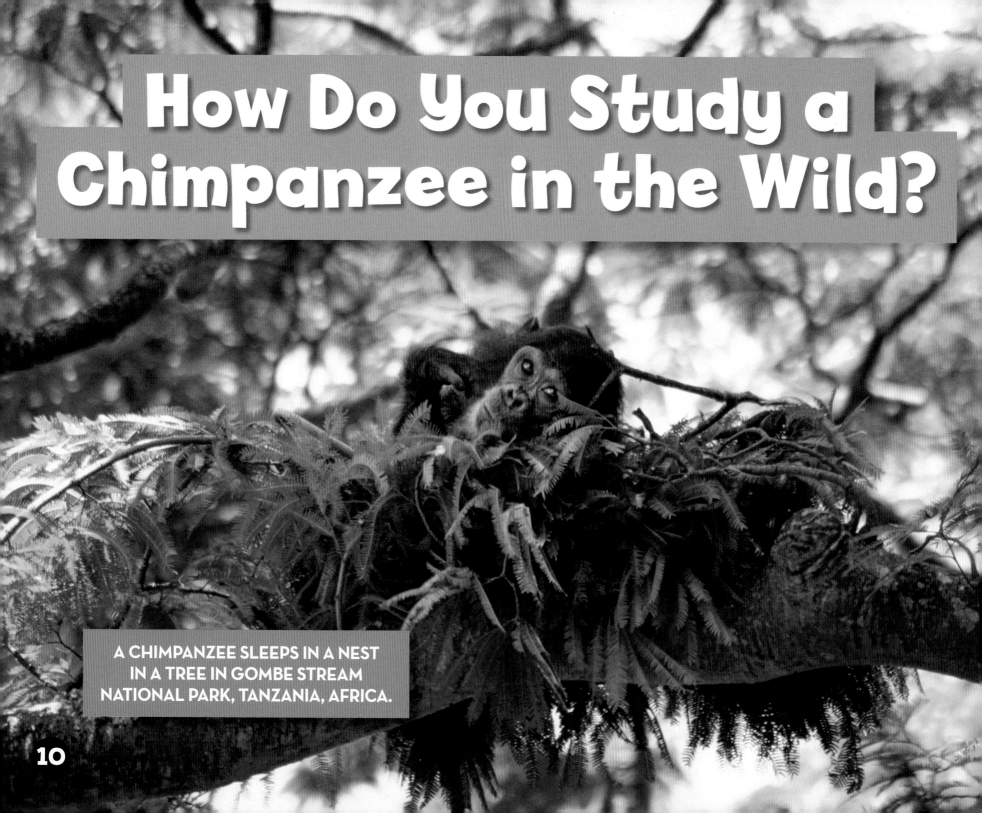

How Do You Study a Chimpanzee in the Wild?

A CHIMPANZEE SLEEPS IN A NEST IN A TREE IN GOMBE STREAM NATIONAL PARK, TANZANIA, AFRICA.

When I'm studying chimps in the field, I leave our camp before the sun comes up to find the chimps before they start their day. If I hear the bulbuls singing, I know I need to hurry.

During the rainy season, the chimps usually snuggle in leafy nests in trees. During the dry season, the trees have lost their leaves, so the chimps sometimes make nests on the ground.

My team and I follow the chimpanzees all day and record what they do.

We take notes on whether the chimps are eating, traveling, or spending time together. We also take notes on how they hunt and how they try to stay cool. During the hot, dry season, the chimps soak in pools of water to cool off, just like humans!

WE TRY NOT TO FOLLOW THE CHIMPS TOO CLOSELY SO THAT WE DON'T DISTURB THEM.

common bulbul

Each field season we have a few questions we want to answer. For example: **What do chimpanzees like to eat? How do they make and use tools for hunting?** We watch the chimps for the answers.

The Fongoli chimps have a big territory—it covers about 40 square miles (104 sq km). That means we do a lot of walking!

When we get home, usually after a 15-hour day, we take a shower by getting a bucket of water from a well. We dip a cup into the water and pour it over our heads. After showering, we eat dinner. My favorite is rice with a sauce made from baobab leaves. Then we go to bed so we can wake up early the next day and do it all over again!

baobab trees

rice

baobab tree fruit

bath bucket

I WATCH THE CHIMPS AND TAKE NOTES ON WHAT THEY'RE DOING.

Does Your Job Ever Get Boring?

During the dry season, the chimpanzees sleep a lot during the day. Do you ever feel tired when it's hot outside? Chimps do, too!

A CHIMPANZEE MOTHER AND BABY REST ON A HOT DAY IN UGANDA, AFRICA.

But most of the time, it's exciting to study chimpanzees. **Watching them is sometimes like watching a movie!** There are chimps who are friends, and chimps who aren't such great friends. Sometimes there are fights. And there is a lot of playing around!

When we're in the field, we have to be alert. **There are dangerous snakes at Fongoli. There are leopards and spotted hyenas that live at Fongoli, too.** But the chimps throw rocks at them to chase them off. It's safer for us when we are with the chimps.

A YOUNG CHIMP PLAYS IN GOMBE STREAM NATIONAL PARK, TANZANIA.

How Do You Get a Wild Chimp to Trust You?

Primatologists who study wild primates usually habituate them. That means we let the animals get used to us. With the Fongoli chimps, it took four years.

First, we found a watering hole and sat on the ground in the shade of a silk cotton tree. In the early afternoon, a group of chimps came to the water to drink. When they saw us, they hid, waiting to see what we'd do. Hours passed, and we sat silently. Then we left. But we came back the next day. And the next. **Finally, they ignored us, which is just what we wanted.**

Some chimps become habituated quickly, like one chimp we named Ross. He was older and spent a lot of time sleeping on a nearby thick vine. Other chimps are shy, like a chimp we named Natasha. She still doesn't like it when film crews come around with their big cameras.

ROSS

NATASHA

Mamadou (MAH-mah-doo),
a high-ranking male, is not shy.
He was the first to "pant-hoot"
and throw branches at us. He's
used to us now, though.

**Once chimps trust you,
you can learn a lot. We've
been studying the Fongoli
chimps for around 20 years.**

MAMADOU

Do the Chimps Remember You?

THIS CHIMP IS PANT-HOOTING.

Most primates can probably recognize people they've seen before, just like you remember people you've met before but might not see too often. For example, I began studying primates by working with chimps at a primate center in Texas. Even many years later, they'd remember me when I'd come back to visit. Sometimes they would pant-hoot or pant-grunt, greeting me like another chimp. The chimpanzees at Fongoli remember me, too.

Because the chimps remember me, I don't need to re-habituate them every field season. I can just start where I left off the last time, watching them and taking notes.

HERE I'M WATCHING A CHIMP, YOPOGON, FROM A SAFE DISTANCE.

What Do Primatologists Bring With Them Into the Field?

When I head to Fongoli to study chimps in the wild, here's what I always take with me.

DATA BOOKS: TO RECORD INFORMATION.

EXTRA HIKING BOOTS: MINE WEAR OUT QUICKLY FROM SO MUCH WALKING! I BRING TWO NEW PAIRS OF HIKING BOOTS WITH ME EACH SEASON.

SNAKE CHAPS: THESE ARE LIKE THE SHIN GUARDS YOU MIGHT WEAR FOR SPORTS. THEY PROTECT MY LEGS FROM SNAKEBITES.

PENS AND PENCILS: I HAVE A SPECIAL PEN FOR WRITING IN THE RAIN.

FIRST AID KIT: I PACK BANDAGES FOR BLISTERS AND MEDICINE IN CASE I'M STUNG BY BEES WHEN THE CHIMPS RAID A HIVE.

FIRST AID

GPS: THIS LETS US RECORD EXACTLY WHERE THE CHIMPS ARE AND HELPS ME FIND MY WAY BACK TO CAMP AT NIGHT.

GPS

Navigate   Options

BINOCULARS: TO HELP ME WATCH THE CHIMPS.

FLASHLIGHTS: I ALWAYS CARRY AT LEAST TWO.

SNACKS: BECAUSE I'M AWAY FROM CAMP FOR A LONG TIME EVERY DAY.

WATER: I ALWAYS CARRY LOTS, ESPECIALLY DURING THE DRY SEASON.

21

Is It Hard to Keep Up With a Chimp?

snub-nosed monkey

Wild primates live in big territories, and they go out in all kinds of weather. So primatologists usually have to be in pretty good shape to follow them. That's especially true with the Fongoli chimps. They walk for miles, so we do, too. Sometimes we follow them through high, wet grass. Other times we follow them through valleys filled with vines and boulders.

Primates spend most of the day foraging for food. But they also spend time grooming each other. For chimps, grooming is more than just keeping clean. It's also soothing and a way to show friendship.

Chimps are acrobatic. Primatologists don't swing from trees, but chimps do!

ONE VERVET MONKEY GROOMS ANOTHER.

A BONOBO SWINGS THROUGH THE TREES.

How Much Do We Know About Primates?

Chimpanzees are probably one of the best studied wild animals alive today, but we keep learning more about them.

We used to think that only humans hunted with tools. But when we started studying the chimps of Fongoli, we learned that they make spears for hunting. It's usually the females who use them.

A CHIMP USES A STICK AS A TOOL TO CATCH TERMITES.

One of the things I'm studying is how these chimps live in their harsh environment.

I want to know how they stay cool. During the dry season, there's not much water for swimming. So the chimps sleep a lot during the day. They wake up for a few hours at night, though, to eat or play. Sometimes I take pictures of them with a special camera that tells me their temperature.

I'm interested in seeing how the chimps grow up and how they change. I wonder who will become more dominant. **I watch the young male chimps, and I try to guess which will be the next alpha, the adult male leader.** In the group of young males I've been watching recently, my guess is that Cy (SIGH) will grow up to be the alpha. He's friendly and also a little naughty.

DAVID, THE ALPHA MALE, COOLS OFF IN A POOL OF WATER.

a picture showing temperature

A GRANDMOTHER AND BABY PLAYING

25

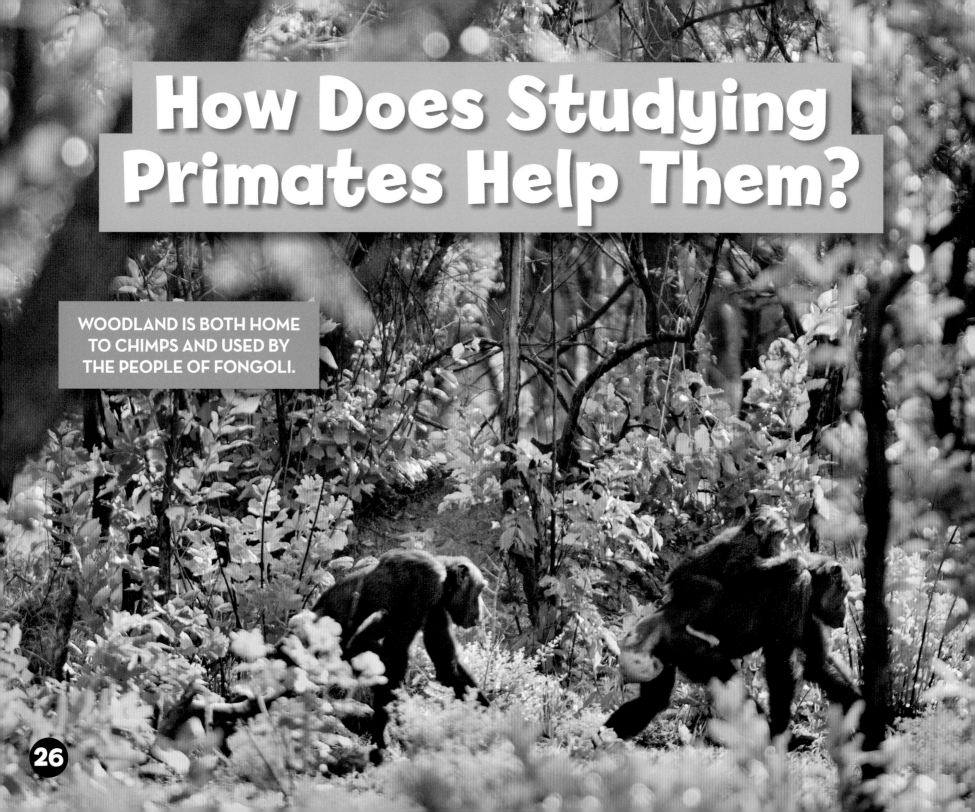

How Does Studying Primates Help Them?

WOODLAND IS BOTH HOME TO CHIMPS AND USED BY THE PEOPLE OF FONGOLI.

Almost all kinds of apes are in danger of extinction. In fact, many kinds of primates are endangered. Studying them and sharing our research can help people think about how we can help protect primates and the places where they live.

For example, when we study how orangutans live in their rainforest home, we can make sure those parts of the rainforest are protected. When we study the kinds of foods primates eat, we can make sure people don't use them up.

BAOBAB FRUIT IS FOOD FOR CHIMPS LIKE BILBO AND HUMANS, TOO.

UNFORTUNATELY, MANY RAINFORESTS ARE CLEARED TO MAKE WAY FOR PALM OIL PLANTATIONS LIKE THIS ONE.

How Do I Become a Primatologist?

Do you want to study primates? Learning about animals will help you get started.

Read! The library is full of books about primates and other animals. The more you learn, the more you'll see how animals are the same and how they are different.

Get outside! Go on a hike and stop to watch the birds and ants and frogs. What do they do? How do they do it?

Watch the animals around you! You can learn a lot from watching the cats and dogs and squirrels that you see every day.

Write it down! As you watch animals, write down what you see in a notebook. I write down whatever I see when I visit Fongoli. I make notes about behaviors I've seen before and new behaviors I want to learn more about.

We've learned many things about primates, but there are so many things left to find out. Maybe you'll be the one to do it!

GLOSSARY

Alpha The animal that is the most powerful or the leader of its group

Behavior How an animal acts, or behaves

Dominant More important or powerful

Dry season A period of dry weather with little rain. In Fongoli, Senegal, the dry season usually lasts from early November to mid-May.

Endangered In danger of extinction

Environment All of the living and nonliving things around an animal

Extinction When a species no longer exists on Earth

Field A site in the wild where a scientist works and researches

Field season The time a scientist spends gathering information in the field each year. It can be a few weeks, a few months, or even an entire year.

Foraging Looking for food

Habituate To cause an animal to become used to, or comfortable with, humans and human-made things

Lemur A small type of primate that lives only on the African island of Madagascar. The most recognizable lemur, the ring-tailed lemur, has a long, striped tail.

Primate A group of animals that includes lemurs, tarsiers, monkeys, and apes. Humans are primates, too! The study of humans and human behavior is called anthropology.

Primatology The study of primates

Rainy season A period of very wet, humid weather with a lot of rain. In Fongoli, Senegal, the rainy season usually lasts from late May to late October.

Sanctuary A place where hurt or captured animals are brought to be healed or protected

Savanna An area that has both grassland and woodland. The African savannas are home to animals like lions and giraffes.

Tarsier A small, nocturnal primate found in Indonesia and the Philippines. Tarsiers are known for their big eyes.

Territory An area where an animal roams and which it protects against intruders

Thatched hut A small building, usually with only one room, and often used as a house. Thatched huts have a roof made of straw or another similar material, called thatching.

Tropics The warm, wet areas of Earth around the Equator

CREDITS

For my parents, Orville and Dorothy,
who instilled in me my love of animals
— J. P.

The author wishes to thank the Republic of Senegal and the people
of the Fongoli area and the book team: Madelyn Rosenberg, text editor;
Shelby Lees, senior editor; Sarah J. Mock, senior photo editor; Kathryn Robbins,
senior designer; Molly Reid, production editor; and Anne LeongSon and
Gus Tello, design production assistants.

Since 1888, the National Geographic Society has funded more
than 12,000 research, exploration, and preservation projects
around the world. The Society receives funds from National
Geographic Partners, LLC, funded in part by your purchase.
A portion of the proceeds from this book supports this vital
work. To learn more, visit natgeo.com/info.

NATIONAL GEOGRAPHIC and Yellow Border Design
are trademarks of the National Geographic Society, used
under license.

For more information, visit nationalgeographic.com,
call 1-877-873-6846, or write to the following address:

National Geographic Partners
1145 17th Street N.W.
Washington, D.C. 20036-4688 U.S.A.

Visit us online at nationalgeographic.com/books

For librarians and teachers: nationalgeographic.com/books
/librarians-and-educators

More for kids from National Geographic: natgeokids.com

National Geographic Kids magazine inspires children to
explore their world with fun yet educational articles on animals,
science, nature, and more. Using fresh storytelling and amazing
photography, *Nat Geo Kids* shows kids ages 6 to 14 the
fascinating truth about the world—and why they should care.
kids.nationalgeographic.com/subscribe

For rights or permissions inquiries, please contact National
Geographic Books Subsidiary Rights: bookrights@natgeo.com

Designed by Kathryn Robbins

Library of Congress Cataloging-in-Publication Data
Names: Pruetz, J. D. (Jill D.), author.
Title: You can be a primatologist / Jill Pruetz.
    Description: Washington, DC : National Geographic Kids,
    [2020] | Series: You can be a ... | Audience: Ages 4-8 |
    Audience: Grades K-1
Identifiers: LCCN 2019034692 | ISBN 9781426337543
    (hardcover) | ISBN 9781426337550 (library binding)
Subjects: LCSH: Primatologists--Vocational guidance--Juvenile
    literature.
Classification: LCC QL737.P9 P755 2020 | DDC
    599.8023--dc23
LC record available at https://lccn.loc.gov/2019034692

Photo Credits:
AL = Alamy Stock Photo; DS = Dreamstime; GI = Getty Images;
NP = Nature Picture Library; SS = Shutterstock

1, Tierfotoagentur/AL; 2-3, Suzi Eszterhas/Minden Pictures; 4-5
(background throughout), Hein Nouwens/SS; 4, Frans Lanting;
5, Martin Harvey/GI; 7 (UP), Nicolette Wackerly; 7 (LO), Frans
Lanting; 8 (LE), Ryan M. Bolton/AL; 8 (RT), Kamonrutm/DS; 9
(UP), Chad Wright/Adobe Stock; 9 (LO), Sergey Uryadnikov/
DS; 10, Danita Delimont/AL; 11 (UP), Courtesy Jill Pruetz; 11 (LO),
Genevieve Vallee/AL; 12 (UP), Dudarev Mikhail/Adobe Stock; 12
(fruit), vainillaychile/Adobe Stock; 12 (rice), zah108/Adobe Stock;
12 (LO), yurakp/Adobe Stock; 13, Tom LaDuke; 14, Suzi Eszterhas/
NP; 15, Anup Shah/NP; 17 (Ross), Frans Lanting; 17 (Natasha),
Nicolette Wackerly; 17 (Mamadou), Courtesy Jill Pruetz; 18, Anup
Shah/NP; 19, Adrien Meguerditchian; 20 (CTR LE), makkayak/
GI; 20 (CTR RT), Sergii Mostovyi/Adobe Stock; 20 (LO RT),
TurtleSkin via Warwick Mills, Inc.; 21 (pen), Petlyaroman/DS; 21
(pencil), Cphoto/DS; 21 (first aid kit), Mega Pixel/SS; 21 (GPS),
Oleksiy Mark/SS; 21 (device), D_V/SS; 21 (water bottle), Kidsada
Manchinda/SS; 21 (flashlight), Moises Fernandez Acosta/SS; 21
(granola), Binh Thanh Bui/SS; 21 (banana), Maks Narodenko/
SS; 21 (raisins), Diana Taliun/SS; 21 (orange), Maks Narodenko/
SS; 21 (binoculars), Nataliya Hora/DS; 22, Staffan Widstrand/
Wild Wonders of China/NP; 23 (LE), Anup Shah/GI; 23 (RT), J
& C Sohns/Picture Press/GI; 24, DLILLC/Corbis/VCG/GI; 25
(UP), Courtesy Jill Pruetz; 25 (CTR), Courtesy Jill Pruetz; 25 (LO),
Anup Shah/NP; 26, Frans Lanting; 27 (UP), Courtesy Jill Pruetz;
27 (LO), Richard Carey/Adobe Stock; 28, kali9/GI; 29 (UP),
biker3/Adobe Stock; 29 (LO), O. Maichle/Adobe Stock; 32, (UP);
Courtesy Jill Pruetz

Printed in Malaysia
20/TWP/1

cover: a young chimpanzee

page 1: a chimpanzee

pages 2–3: an orangutan

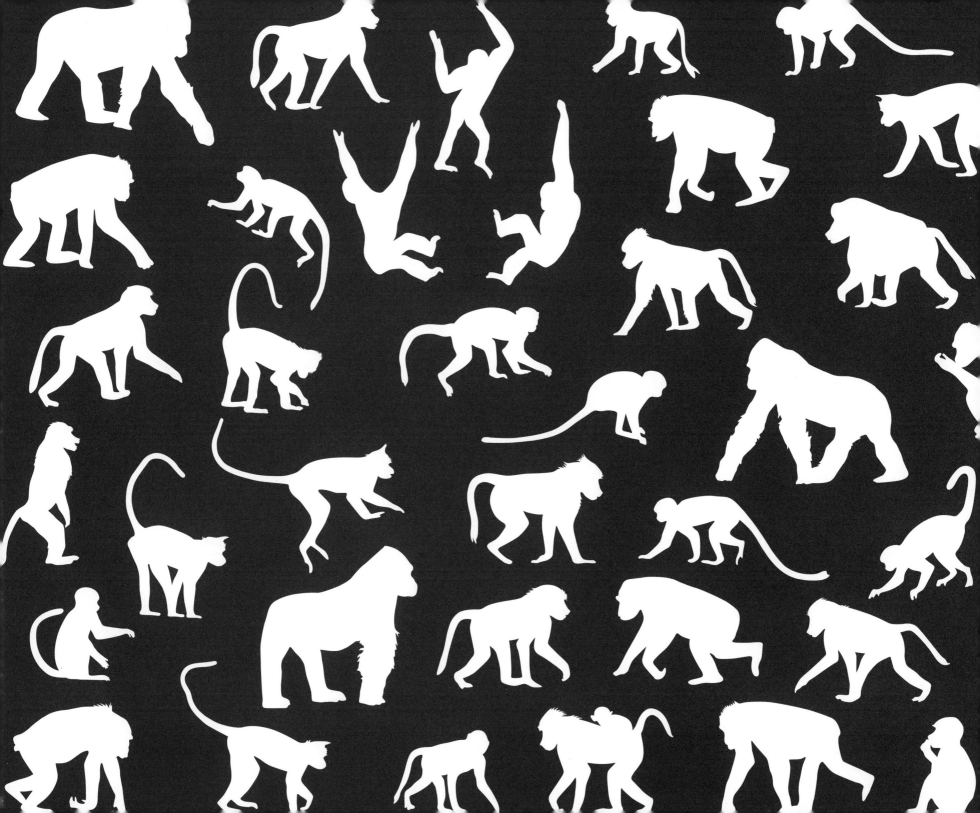

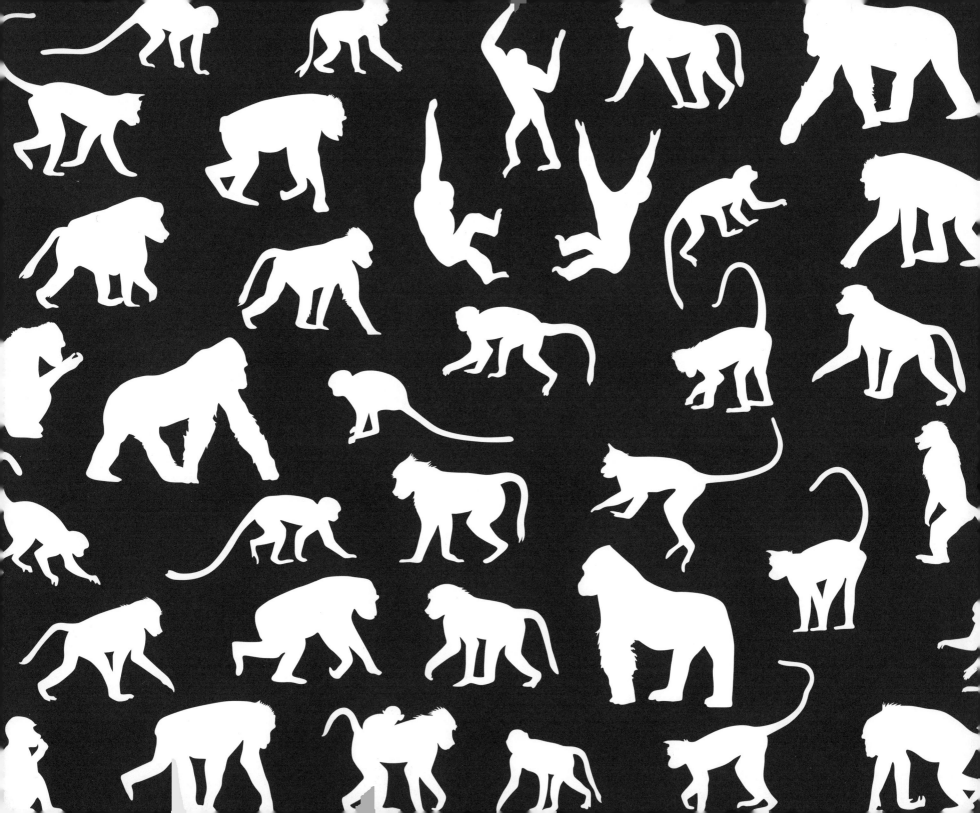